posh®
Coloring
BOOK

· · · · · · · · · ·

GOD IS GOOD
Deborah Muller

· · · · · · · · · ·

Andrews McMeel
Publishing®
a division of Andrews McMeel Universal

POSH® COLORING BOOK
GOD IS GOOD

Andrews McMeel Publishing
a division of Andrews McMeel Universal
1130 Walnut Street, Kansas City, Missouri 64106

www.andrewsmcmeel.com

16 17 18 19 20 SHZ 10 9 8 7 6 5 4 3 2 1

ISBN: 978-1-4494-7800-1

ATTENTION: SCHOOLS AND BUSINESSES
Andrews McMeel books are available at quantity discounts with
bulk purchase for educational, business, or sales promotional use.
For information, please e-mail the Andrews McMeel Publishing
Special Sales Department: specialsales@amuniversal.com.

God's plans will always be greater than all your disappointments.

Be brave enough to hold on to hope that life will be beautiful again.

Forgive

It heals the heart, mind, body, and spirit.

I WILL NOT FALL

Psalm 46:5

Let us approach God's throne of grace with confidence, so that we may receive mercy and grace.

by His grace

Hebrews 4:16

Infallible
Faithful
reliable
Worthy
Steadfast

That's my GOD.

Just Do It! EZRA 10:4

RISE UP TAKE COURAGE

Believe & Receive

Mark 11:24

When you go through deep water I will be with you. ISAIAH 43:2

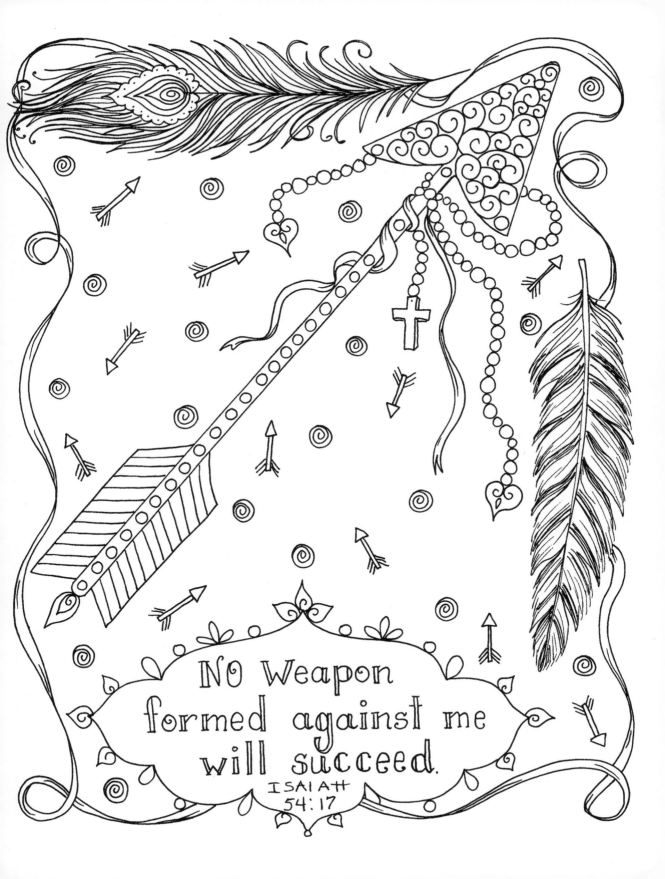

God gives us Peace in our hearts

Colossians 3:15

LOVE · HEALING · PEACE · HOPE

FAITH · HOPE · BLESSINGS · GRACE · JOY · LOVE

MERCY · PEACE · GOODNESS · FAITH

HEALING · GRACE

HEALING · FAITH · MERCY · JOY · LOVE

STANDING on the PROMISES of GOD

it's kind of FUN to do the impossible

with God all things are possible. matthew 19:26

Let the Lover of your Soul restore it.

PSALM 23:3

Perfect Love casts out fear. 1 JOHN 4:18

GOD

surrounds me with HIS favor

You surround me with your favor. Psalm 5:12

DON'T BE AFRAID JUST BELIEVE

MARK 5:36

heal

⭐ let it go

⭐ forgive

⭐ move forward

Be tolerant and forgive each other. Just as the Lord forgave you. Colossians 3:13

1 John 4:16

God is love

do not be afraid to SOAR

Psalm 9:1

I will give thanks

with my whole Heart

there is Joy ahead

1 Peter 1:6

You silence the noise of the seas and give me Peace
Psalm 65:7

Trust Him

god is working it all out for good.

ROMANS 8:28

There
are far
better things
ahead
than any
we leave
behind.

C. S. LEWIS

The future depends on what you do today

When God closes a door He opens a window

Thank you, God, for closing doors I'm not strong enough to close... and for new adventures.

LIVE EVERY DAY WITH INTENT!

GOD will give us the desires of our HEARTS

He is always with me

I am with you Always!

matthew 28:20

The Lord is my Light and my Salvation

Psalm 27:1

Above All, Love each other deeply

1 Peter 4:8